DIEGO RIVERA
HIS WORLD AND OURS

DUNCAN TONATIUH

Abrams Books for Young Readers
New York

To my Dad, the first artist I met,
the one who always inspires me
—D. T.

The artwork in this book was hand-drawn, then collaged digitally.

Library of Congress Cataloging-in-Publication Data

Tonatiuh, Duncan.
Diego Rivera his world and ours / by Duncan Tonatiuh.
p. cm.
Includes bibliographical references.
ISBN 978-0-8109-9731-8 (alk. paper)
1. Rivera, Diego, 1886–1957—Juvenile literature. 2. Painters—Mexico—Biography—
Juvenile literature. 1. Rivera, Diego, 1886–1957. II. Title.
ND259.R5T57 2011
759.972—dc22
[B]
2010032618

Text and illustrations copyright © 2011 Duncan Tonatiuh
Page 33: *The Great City of Tenochtitlán [La gran ciudad de Tenochtitlán]*, by Diego Rivera. © 2010 Banco de
México Diego Rivera Frida Kahlo Museums Trust, Mexico, D.F. / Artists Rights Society (ARS), New York
Book design by Melissa Arnst

Printed and bound in China
10 9 8 7 6 5 4 3 2 1

Abrams Books for Young Readers are available at special discounts when purchased in quantity for
premiums and promotions as well as fundraising or educational use. Special editions can also be
created to specification. For details, contact specialmarkets@abramsbooks.com or the address below.

THE ART OF BOOKS SINCE 1949
115 West 18th Street
New York, NY 10011
www.abramsbooks.com

Diego Rivera was born in Mexico in a city called Guanajuato, which means the "land of frogs." As a boy Diego enjoyed playing with his trains, but more than anything he liked to draw.

Diego loved drawing so much that when he was a young man he sailed on a ship across the ocean. He went to the city of Madrid in Spain to study art under the direction of a well-known painter. There he learned the classical way to paint, which means his finished paintings looked very realistic, almost like photographs.

After his studies, Diego went to Paris, the capital of France. There he met young artists who were painting in new and exciting ways. He experimented with these new methods of painting himself. One method was called Cubism, in which the painting did not exactly resemble its subject but was composed of geometric shapes, such as squares, circles, and triangles.

One day a politician named José Vasconcelos urged Diego to return to Mexico. He wanted Diego and other artists to paint murals around the city about the Mexican people's history and customs. Diego was thrilled by this new project.

When he returned to his homeland, Diego traveled through its deserts, mountains, and jungles. He wanted to be inspired by his country. He met people who worked the land, and he visited the ruins of ancient Mexican civilizations, like those of the Aztecs and the Maya.

Diego was full of ideas after his trips. With the help of friends and apprentices, he began to paint murals on large walls so that everyone in his country—rich and poor, young and old—could see and learn from them.

In his murals, Diego combined the classical way of painting he had learned as a young man and the new styles of art he had experimented with abroad. But he merged them with the simple yet elegant forms of ancient Mexican art that he had grown passionate for after his travels.

On the walls of an important government building,
Diego painted the history of his country. He painted
the struggle of the Mexican people to break free
from the Spanish king.

He also painted the fight that took place many
years later when farmers and workers defended
themselves against greedy men who were taking
advantage of them.

Diego painted his country's dances and traditions, such as *La Zandunga*, a love dance from the coastal area, and the dance of *los listones*, a ribbon dance from the south.

He wanted to celebrate the things that were special to Mexico and wanted Mexicans, from all distant parts of the land, to learn about their culture and feel proud.

Diego lived to be an old man. By the time he passed away, he had created many wonderful artworks and was celebrated by people in Mexico as well as around the world.

But if he were alive today, what would he paint?
Would he paint the way we dress and live?
Would he paint the way we play?

Would he paint the big city . . .

Or would he paint students at their desks . . .

. . . as he painted street vendors selling *flores.*

. . . just as he painted the Aztec warriors fighting the invading soldiers, the Spanish *conquistadores*?

Would Diego paint our craze for monsters
and creatures from outer space . . .

... as he painted the god Quetzalcoatl,
the feathered serpent?

Diego's murals teach us about the past. But they also show a better future for common people. Diego imagined everyone—men and women, boys and girls, of all ages and nationalities—living together and caring for one another.

Today Diego is not around to make this happen. So it is up to us to make our own murals and bring them to life.

GLOSSARY OF WORDS AND REFERENCES IN STORY SEQUENCE

"Classical way to paint": The manner of painting held to be correct and proper by most people at a given period of time. During Diego Rivera's early life it was usually held to be a form of painting where the final artwork looks like the subject, whether a photograph or an impression or feeling.

Cubism: A method of painting and sculpture developed in Paris in the early twentieth century, characterized by making natural forms (people, animals, plants, etc.) into abstract, often geometric structures.

Mural: Any piece of artwork painted directly on a wall, ceiling, or other large permanent surface.

History: Usually a chronological record of events, as of the life or development of a people or country or institution.

Custom: A practice followed by people of a particular group or region, such as shaking hands to say "hello."

Aztecs: A Mexican Indian people who built an empire, centered on the Valley of Mexico, that was overthrown by Spanish invaders in the early sixteenth century.

Maya: A Meso-American indigenous people inhabiting southeast Mexico, Guatemala, and Belize whose civilization reached its height around 300–900 CE. They are noted for their architecture, city planning, mathematics, calendar, and hieroglyphic writing system.

Apprentice: One who is learning a trade or occupation from a master in the field.

"Ancient Mexican art": Pottery and other works by the Aztec and Mayan people.

"Painted the struggle of the Mexican people to break free from the Spanish king": The Mexican War of Independence (1810–1821) was fought by the people of Mexico, who sought independence from Spain. Mexico had been under Spanish control since the Spanish conquest of the Aztec Empire in the 1500s.

"Painted the fight that took place many years later when farmers and workers defended themselves": The Mexican Revolution (1910–c. 1920) was brought on by several things, among them, tremendous disagreement among the Mexican people over the dictatorship of President Porfirio Díaz. During his thirty years in office, power was in the hands of a select few; the people had no power to express their opinions or select their public officials. Wealth was likewise controlled by a small group of people. Common people in both the cities and the countryside were subjected to many injustices.

Tradition: A ritual passed down from one generation to the next, such as a dance or how to celebrate a holiday.

La Zandunga, or La Sandunga: A song and a genre of Mexican folk music. It comes from the Tehuantepec region, which encompasses parts of the modern-day states of Oaxaca, Veracruz, Tabasco, and Chiapas.

Los listones: In Spanish listones means "ribbons." The ribbon dance, or danza de los listones, is a traditional dance from the modern state of Yucatán.

Tenochtitlán: The capital city of the Aztecs, located in what is today Mexico City.

Production line: A manufacturing method in which people or machines are each responsible for one part of assembling a product, which is then passed to the next person or machine to add a different part, until the product is completely assembled.

Street vendors: People who sell their wares—food, clothes, flowers, etc.—in public areas outdoors.

Flores: Flowers

Luchadores: Professional Mexican wrestlers who wear colorful masks. Their sport involves varied techniques and moves.

Spanish conquistadores: Spanish soldiers

Quetzalcoatl: A Meso-American deity, especially of the Aztecs, whose name comes from the Nahuatl language and means "feathered serpent."

AUTHOR'S NOTE

Diego Rivera was born in the city of Guanajuato in 1886. From a young age he showed an exceptional ability to draw. He received his first artistic training at the San Carlos Academy when his family moved to Mexico City. He excelled, and when he was twenty-one years old he was awarded a scholarship by the governor of Veracruz to travel to Madrid, Spain, to study with the painter Eduardo Chicharro. Rivera spent the next fourteen years in Europe. He lived in Spain, France, and Italy. In Paris he met and mingled with the artistic vanguard. He was influenced by such painters as Paul Cézanne and Pablo Picasso and became an accomplished Cubist painter. In Italy he saw the work of the Renaissance painters, including Giotto and Piero della Francesca.

Rivera's career took a dramatic turn when José Vasconcelos, the Mexican government's secretary of education, asked him to be a part of the major murals program he was launching. In 1921 Rivera returned to Mexico. He was encouraged to travel around the country with other painters. Vasconcelos wanted the murals to be about Mexican history and the Mexican people. The nation had just experienced the Mexican Revolution.

Rivera painted his first mural in 1922 at the National Preparatory School and his second one from 1922 to 1928 at the Secretariat of Public Education, both of them in Mexico City. While painting these murals Rivera developed his own unique style, the one that has come to identify him. In his artwork Rivera combined the aesthetics and techniques of Renaissance frescoes, the experimentation and space compression of Cubism, and the boldness, roundness, and geometry of Mexican Pre-Columbian art that he had come to admire.

Over the next twenty-five years Rivera worked on more than twelve major mural projects, sometimes involving entire chapels and multiple floors and walls. Many of his murals are in Mexico City, but a number of them are in the United States, in such places as Detroit and San Francisco. He was very prolific and also painted an incredible number of canvases and watercolors up until his death in 1957.

Rivera was a multifaceted and often controversial person. It is hard to do justice to all the different aspects of his life. He was, among other things, a lover of science and technology, an avid Pre-Columbian art collector, and the husband of the famous painter Frida Kahlo.

I have had the opportunity to see several of Rivera's murals in Mexico City. They are luminescent, monumental, and formally exquisite, and they tackle epic subjects including the Spanish conquest of Mexico and the Mexican Revolution.

What I admire most about Rivera is the way in which he looked back at the art of ancient Mexico and was able to incorporate some of its aesthetic into his own work. He combined that ancient art with the art of the modern era and was able to create something new and exciting, but also relevant to an entire nation.

In my artwork I look back to ancient Mexican art also. I combine these ancient art styles with the art of the digital era. I remember standing on the stairs of the National Palace in Mexico, looking at Rivera's mural and thinking, what would he paint nowadays? What would he paint in the world of cell phones and the web 2.0? And with that thought this book was ignited.

SOME OF THE PLACES WHERE YOU CAN FIND
THE WORK OF DIEGO RIVERA

UNITED STATES

Arizona State University Art Museum, Tempe
Art Institute of Chicago, Illinois
Arthur Ross Gallery at the University of Pennsylvania,
    Philadelphia
Brooklyn Museum, New York City
Cleveland Museum of Art, Ohio
Indianapolis Museum of Art, Indiana
Ball State University Museum of Art, Muncie, Indiana
Dallas Museum of Art, Texas
Detroit Institute of Arts, Michigan
Fine Arts Museum of San Francisco, California
Library of Congress, Washington, D.C.
Metropolitan Museum of Art, New York City
Mildred Lane Kemper Art Museum, St. Louis, Missouri
Museum of Modern Art, New York City
National Gallery of Art, Washington, D.C.
Philadelphia Museum of Art, Pennsylvania
San Diego Museum of Art, California
San Francisco Museum of Modern Art, California

OUTSIDE THE UNITED STATES

Birmingham Museums and Art Gallery, England
Tate Modern, London, England
Virtual Museum of Canada, http://www.museevirtuel-
    virtualmuseum.ca

Many of Diego Rivera's murals are found in Mexico at
locations too numerous to list here.

BIBLIOGRAPHY

Downs, Linda Bank. *Diego Rivera: The Detroit Industry Murals.*
New York: W. W. Norton & Company, 1999.

Hamill, Pete. *Diego Rivera.* New York: Harry N. Abrams, 1999.

Kettenmann, Andrea. *Diego Rivera, 1886–1957: A
Revolutionary Spirit in Modern Art.* New York: Taschen, 1997.

Rivera, Diego. *My Art, My Life: An Autobiography.* With Gladys
March. New York: Dover Publications, 1992.

Rivera, Juan Coronel, Luis-Martín Lozano, Augustín Arteaga, and
William Robinson. *Diego Rivera, Art and Revolution.* Mexico City
Instituto Nacional de Bellas Artes / Landucci Editores, 1999.

Rochfort, Desmond. *Mexican Muralists Orozco, Rivera,
Siqueiros.* San Francisco: Chronicle Books, 1998.

Wolfe, Bertram David. *The Fabulous Life of Diego Rivera.* New
York: Stein and Day, 1963.

Websites

http://www.abcgallery.com/R/rivera/rivera.html
http://diegorivera.com/
http://www.riveramural.com
http://www.sep.gob.mx/
http://catarina.udlap.mx/